Date: 9/17/12

MUSTANGS

Meryl Magby

PowerKiDS
press

New York

American
ANIMALS

Published in 2012 by The Rosen Publishing Group, Inc.
29 East 21st Street, New York, NY 10010

First Edition

Editor: Amelie von Zumbusch
Book Design: Ashley Drago

Photo Credits: Cover, p. 18 Eastcott Momatiuk/Getty Images; pp. 4–5, 9 (bottom) Shutterstock.com; p. 6 Hulton Collection/Getty Images; p. 7 Tom Till/Getty Images; p. 8 © www.iStockphoto.com/Jim Parkin; pp. 9 (top), 16, 19 iStockphoto/Thinkstock; p. 10 © www.iStockphoto.com/Randy Harris; p. 11 (left) © www.iStockphoto.com/Ivanastar; p. 11 (right) Fuse/Getty Images; pp. 12–13 © www.iStockphoto.com/Missing35mm; p. 14 Melissa Farlow/Getty Images; p. 15 Hemera/Thinkstock; p. 17 © www.iStockphoto.com/Cynthia Baldauf; p. 20 Jeff T. Green/Getty Images; p. 21 Gary Alvis/ Getty Images; p. 22 © www.iStockphoto.com/karenparker2000.

Library of Congress Cataloging-in-Publication Data

Magby, Meryl.
 Mustangs / by Meryl Magby. — 1st ed.
      p. cm. — (American animals)
 Includes index.
 ISBN 978-1-4488-6178-1 (library binding) — ISBN 978-1-4488-6315-0 (pbk.) —
ISBN 978-1-4488-6316-7 (6-pack)
 1. Mustang—Juvenile literature. I. Title.
 SF293.M9M34 2012
 599.665'5—dc23
                                        2011027119

Manufactured in the United States of America

CPSIA Compliance Information: Batch #WW12PK: For Further Information contact Rosen Publishing, New York, New York at 1-800-237-9932

Contents

The Mighty Mustang

Most people do not think of horses as wild animals. However, in some parts of the western United States, herds of wild horses roam the land. These horses are called mustangs. Mustangs are **feral** horses. This means that although mustangs are wild animals now, they were not always wild. Their **ancestors** were horses that ran away from their owners or were let go many years ago.

These mustangs are in Colorado. Mustangs also live in Arizona, California, Idaho, Montana, Nevada, New Mexico, Oregon, Utah, and Wyoming.

Mustangs have been called a **symbol** of the spirit of the West. This is because mustangs have an important place in the history of the western United States. However, there are only about 38,000 mustangs living in the wild today.

Horses in North America

Many of the horses used by Native Americans in the West were related to the mustangs that roam the western United States today.

Wild horses lived in North America millions of years ago. However, they died out about 10,000 years ago. Horses returned to North America about 500 years ago when Spanish explorers brought them from Europe to Mexico. In time, the use of horses by people spread all over North America. Horses helped both Native Americans and European settlers travel, hunt, and carry things more easily.

Horses often escaped from their owners into the wild. People who could not feed their horses often let them go into the wild as well. By the 1800s, there were about two million feral horses in the American West.

Mustang Habitats

These mustangs are part of the Pryor Mountain herd.

Mustangs once could be found all over the western United States. Today, wild mustangs live on more than 30 million acres (12 million ha) of public lands in 10 different states. More than half of these mustangs live in Nevada.

Mustangs live in several **habitats**, or kinds of land. Some live on flat, grassy plains. Others live in drier desert areas or in rocky mountain areas. One group of mustangs, called the Pryor Mountain herd, lives in a hard-to-reach mountain area near the border of Montana and Wyoming. This herd has not mixed with other mustang herds for over 200 years.

Mustangs live in several North American deserts. These include Black Rock Desert in Nevada, Red Desert in Utah, and parts of the Mojave Desert in California.

These feral horses live in Theodore Roosevelt National Park, in North Dakota. The park is home to a herd of about 70 to 110 horses.

A Mix of Many Breeds

At one time, many mustangs were closely related to the Spanish, or Iberian, horses brought to North America by Spanish explorers. Today, most mustangs also have ancestors from other horse **breeds**, or types. These horses escaped or were let go into the wild over the years. The breeds include Thoroughbreds, Morgans, and Arabians.

Pryor Mountain mustangs are still very closely related to Iberian horses. They tend

Like all horses, mustangs have a good sense of smell. They also see and hear very well.

Mustang coats can be many different colors. The animals can also have several different kinds of markings.

to be smaller than other mustangs. This means that they need to eat less food to fuel their bodies. They also have certain markings, such as zebra stripes on their legs and black lines down the middles of their backs.

All horses have manes. A mane is a line of long hair that grows along the back of a horse's head and neck.

11

Mustang Facts

1. The back of Nevada's state quarter shows three mustangs galloping in front of mountains. Many of Nevada's mustangs live in the Great Basin, an area with many mountains and deserts.

2. The word "mustang" comes from the Spanish word *mesteno*. At one time, this word meant "wild or unclaimed sheep." However, it has come to mean "wild horse."

3. Like the Pryor Mountain herd, Kiger mustangs from Steens Mountain, in southeastern Oregon, are closely related to Spanish horses. Many of these mustangs have **dun** coats and zebra stripes on their back legs.

4. In the 1950s, a woman from Nevada named Velma B. Johnston worked to keep people from rounding up mustangs on public lands. This helped mustangs become **protected** by the government. Her nickname was Wild Horse Annie.

5. Mustangs do not have many natural **predators**, or animals that hunt them, left in the wild. However, mountain lions sometimes hunt young mustangs because they are slower and weaker than adult mustangs.

6. Wild mustangs often live together in small family groups. Mustangs in the same family group **groom** each other, or care for each other's coats, manes, and tails.

Grazing and Foraging

These mustangs are gathered around a water hole, or low place in the ground where water pools. Mustangs also drink from streams and springs.

Like all other horses, mustangs are **herbivores**. This means they eat only plants. Mustangs eat mostly grass. They **graze**, or eat grass, throughout the day. Mustangs will also eat other plants, such as shrubs, if they cannot find any grass to eat.

Mustangs most often look for water to drink in the later part of the day. Bands of mustangs often drink together at natural springs, streams, and lakes. In the summer months, it may be hard for mustangs to find enough water to drink. When it gets very cold in the winter, they often eat snow instead of drinking water.

Mustangs eat many kinds of grass, such as bluebunch wheatgrass, needlegrass, and Indian ricegrass.

Herds and Bands

The land that a mustang wanders over is its **range**. A large group of mustangs that shares the same range is called a herd. However, mustangs often live in smaller family groups of between 5 and 15 horses. These groups are called bands. There are many bands in a herd.

Mustangs and other horses groom each other with their teeth.

Most mustang bands are led by one male horse, called a stallion. The other mustangs in the band are adult female horses, called mares, and young mustangs, called foals. The stallion keeps the mares and foals safe. One of the mares leads the band to food and water or away from danger.

Growing Up

Stallions and mares mate in the late spring. Mares give birth to their babies the next spring, about 11 months later. After it turns a year old, a male foal is called a colt. A one-year-old female foal is called a filly.

Young mustangs leave their parents to form new bands when they are two

Mustang foals can stand just a few hours after they are born.

A mother mustang most often goes off on her own to give birth. A few days after the foal is born, the mother and foal go back to their band.

or three years old. However, young stallions sometimes cannot find mares with which to mate. When this happens, the stallions form their own bands and roam the plains to look for mates. Young stallions sometimes fight for mares with older stallions.

Protecting Mustangs

These mustangs are being put up for adoption by the BLM. The people gathered to look at the horses hope to give them new homes.

Mustangs used to be rounded up by ranchers who wanted their livestock to eat the grass that mustangs were eating. Then, in 1971, Congress passed the Wild Free-Roaming Horses and Burros Act. It protects mustangs from being caught or killed by ranchers. However, it also limits the number of mustangs that can stay in the wild.

The Bureau of Land Management (BLM) is in charge of making sure the number of mustangs in the wild does not get too large. Every year, the BLM rounds up between 5,000 and 10,000 mustangs. Some of these mustangs are sold in **auctions**. Others are put up for adoption.

The man on horseback is rounding up these mustangs. People sometimes use helicopters to round up mustangs. They train horses to lead mustangs into fenced-in areas, too.

The Future for Mustangs

One place to see mustangs is in mustang **sanctuaries**. These are places where mustangs that were rounded up by the BLM but are not sold or adopted can live.

People disagree on how mustangs should be managed. Some people are against the BLM rounding up mustangs at all. Others think that the BLM's actions keep herds healthy. All mustang lovers are happy that the horses are no longer in danger of dying out, though. These horses will remain a living symbol of the West for years to come.

These mustangs live at the Black Hills Wild Horse Sanctuary. The sanctuary is near Hot Springs, South Dakota.

Glossary

ancestors (AN-ses-terz) Relatives that lived long ago.

auctions (OK-shunz) Sales at which goods are sold to whoever pays the most.

breeds (BREEDZ) Groups of animals that look alike and have the same relatives.

dun (DUN) A brownish gray horse coat color that includes markings such as a dark stripe down the back.

feral (FER-al) An animal that used to live with people but that has gone back to the wild.

graze (GRAYZ) To feed on grass.

groom (GROOM) To clean one's body and make it neat.

habitats (HA-buh-tats) The kinds of land where animals or plants naturally live.

herbivores (ER-buh-vorz) Animals that eat only plants.

predators (PREH-duh-terz) Animals that kill other animals for food.

protected (pruh-TEK-ted) Kept safe.

range (RAYNJ) The distance something can travel.

sanctuaries (SANK-choo-weh-reez) Places where people or animals are kept safe.

symbol (SIM-bul) An object or a picture that stands for something else.

Index

Web Sites

Due to the changing nature of Internet links, PowerKids Press has developed an online list of Web sites related to the subject of this book. This site is updated regularly. Please use this link to access the list:
www.powerkidslinks.com/aman/mustang/

24